SPORTS' GREATEST RIVALRIES

LAKERS vs. CELTICS

Parker Holmes

PowerKiDS press

New York

Published in 2014 by The Rosen Publishing Group, Inc.
29 East 21st Street, New York, NY 10010

Copyright © 2014 by The Rosen Publishing Group, Inc.

All rights reserved. No part of this book may be reproduced in any form without permission in writing from the publisher, except by a reviewer.

First Edition

Editor: Dean Galiano
Book Design: Julie Zerbib

Photo Credits: Front Cover, back cover (front, top)Joan Adlen/Getty Images; (front, bottom) John W. McDonough/Sports Illustrated/Getty Images; (back, top) Jim Rogash/Getty Images; (back, bottom) Robert Riger/Getty Images; Stephen Dunn/Getty Images; Richard Mackson/Sports Illustrated/Getty Images; Christian Peterson/Getty Images; p. 1, 20, 21 John Biever/ Sports Illustrated/Getty Images; p. 4 (background photo) 7, 8, 15, 17, 22, 24 John W. McDonough/Sports Illustrated/Getty Images; p. 5 Stephen Dunn/Getty Images; p. 6 (left) Jim Rogash/Getty Images; (middle) Kevin Winter/Getty Images; (right) Ronald Martinez/Getty Images; p. 11 Robert Riger/Getty Images; p. 12 (left) Richard Mackson/Sports Illustrated/Getty Images; (center) Rick Stewart/Allsport/Getty Images; p. 13 Rick Stewart/Getty Images; p. 15 Richard Mackson/Sports Illustrated/Getty Images; p. 17 Christian Peterson/Getty Images; p. 18 (left) Kathryn E. McDonald/US Navy/Getty Images; (center) Karl Walter/Getty Images; p. 19 Stephen Dunn/Getty Images.

Library of Congress Cataloging-in-Publication Data

Holmes, Parker.
 Lakers vs. Celtics / by Parker Holmes. -- First edition.
    pages cm. -- (Sports' Greatest Rivalries)
 Includes index.
 ISBN 978-1-4777-2785-0 (library binding) -- ISBN 978-1-4777-2786-7 (pbk.) -- ISBN 978-1-4777-2787-4 (6-pack)
 1. Los Angeles Lakers (Basketball team)--History--Juvenile literature. 2. Boston Celtics (Basketball team)--History--Juvenile literature. 3. Sports' Greatest Rivalries--United States. I. Title.
 GV885.52.L67H65 2014
 796.323'64--dc23

2013010304

Manufactured in the United States of America

CPSIA Compliance Information: Batch #W13PK5: For Further Information contact Rosen Publishing, New York, New York at 1-800-237-9932

CONTENTS

Basketball's Best Rivalry 4
Celtic Pride 6
Showtime Lakers 8
The 1960s: A Dynasty 10
The 1980s: Magic and Bird 12
The Magic Show 14
A New Era 16
East vs. West 18
Celtics vs. Lakers Timeline 20
Celtics-Lakers Head-to-Head 22
Glossary 23
Index 24
Websites 24

BASKETBALL'S BEST RIVALRY

The Celtics versus the Lakers: it's the greatest **rivalry** in basketball. The Boston Celtics and the Los Angeles Lakers have faced each other in championship finals more than any other two teams in the National Basketball Association (NBA). There have been many great moments in the series—Larry Bird versus Magic Johnson, buzzer-beating shots, and thrilling overtime victories. When these two teams play, it's the **ultimate** East Coast versus West Coast showdown.

In regular season play, Boston has a slightly better record. From their first meeting in 1948 through the 2012-13 season, the Celtics have won 154 times, and the Lakers have won 124. Boston also has the lead in championship finals. They've played each other in 12 finals, and the Celtics have won 9. Victories in the series never come easy. With these two rivals, the competition is always intense!

Kobe Bryant drives around Jason Terry in a 2013 game. These two teams have been playing hard against each other for more than 60 years.

CELTIC PRIDE

The Celtics have won 17 championships. That's more than any other NBA team. A cast of great players have helped the Celtics win titles, including Bill Russell, Larry Bird, Kevin Garnett, and many others dating back to the team's early years. Located in Boston, Massachusetts, the Celtics started playing ball in 1946.

The Celtics are well known for their winking leprechaun logo.
Bill Russell (at right) may be the greatest defensive player of all time.

Celtics forward Paul Pierce dribbles down the court during the 2010 finals. The Celtics have won more finals than any other team.

Do you know where the name "Celtics" comes from? Many **centuries** ago, a group of people known as the Celts lived in Europe. Many of these Celtic people lived in Ireland. The Celtics is a fitting name for the team because many Irish **immigrants** have lived in Boston. The team **logo** is a picture of a leprechaun, which is an Irish **mythical** creature. The team's main color is green. Green is an Irish national color.

SHOWTIME LAKERS

The Lakers are one of the NBA's most famous teams. Many of the sport's greatest players have played for the Lakers. These stars have led the Lakers to 16 championships. How many Lakers stars can you name? A few of the most famous are Magic Johnson, Kareem Abdul-Jabbar, Shaquille O'Neal, and Kobe Bryant.

The Lakers haven't always played in Los Angeles. They started playing in 1947 in Minneapolis, Minnesota. Minnesota is known as the "Land of 10,000 Lakes," and this is how the team got its name. The team kept the name even after it moved to Los Angeles, California, in 1960.

The Lakers play in the NBA's Western Conference. They have won a record 32 Western Conference titles. The team that wins the Western Conference goes on to play the Eastern Conference champion in the finals.

Kobe Bryant (#8) and Shaquille O'Neal (#34) played eight seasons together in Los Angeles. The Lakers won three straight finals from 2000 to 2002.

THE 1960s: A DYNASTY

The rivalry between the Celtics and Lakers really heated up in the 1960s. They faced each other six times in the finals during that **decade**. The teams played some very close games, but the Celtics won every title. Boston was the NBA's **dominant** team of the 1960s. In fact, the Celtics of the 1960s may have been the most dominant **dynasty** in sports history.

The Lakers came very close to winning the 1962 finals. They had a strong team with stars such as Jerry West, Frank Selvy, and Elgin Baylor. The championship came down to a seventh and final game. With only a few seconds left, the score was tied, 100–100.

The Lakers had final possession of the ball, and Frank Selvy had time for one last shot to win the title. Selvy took an open jump shot, but the ball bounced off the rim. The game went to overtime, and the Celtics won 110–107. Los Angeles would have to wait to get their **revenge**.

Bill Russell (#6) goes up to block a shot against the Lakers in the early 1960s. Russell's great defensive skills helped the Celtics dominate the NBA.

THE 1980s: MAGIC AND BIRD

The rivalry heated up again in the 1980s, and it was made even hotter by the competition between Laker Magic Johnson and Celtic Larry Bird. These two superstars loved to beat each other! In 1984, the two players got to meet in the finals for the first time. It was a tough, exciting series. Bird played especially well in the series, and the Celtics came out on top.

Larry Bird (center) drives through the defense of Magic Johnson (right) and Kevin Grevey during the '85 finals. Bird (right) is one of the best shooters in history.

12

Lakers center Kareem Abdul-Jabbar (center, looking at the camera) scored more points than any player in NBA history.

    The Lakers got another chance against Boston in the finals the next year. The Lakers' center, Kareem Abdul-Jabbar, was near the end of his career, but he proved that his famous skyhook shot was still a powerful weapon. Abdul-Jabbar, Magic, and the rest of the Lakers finally took down their arch-rivals. They beat Boston in the finals for the first time. Lakers fans were thrilled to finally come out on top.

THE MAGIC SHOW

Two years after their 1985 title, the Lakers again met the Celtics in the finals. Los Angeles won two of the first three games. Boston **desperately** needed to win the fourth game to even up the series.

During that fourth game, Boston led, 106–105, with only a few seconds left. Then Magic Johnson got the ball, drove toward the basket, and swished a skyhook shot over the outstretched arms of Celtics defenders.

Los Angeles led, 107–106, with 2 seconds left. The Celtics had time for one last shot. Boston had its best player, Larry Bird, take the final shot. Bird threw up a three-point shot that looked good in the air. The fans were holding their breath. But then—clank—the ball bounced off the rim, barely missing. The Lakers won the game and went on to win the title!

Magic Johnson goes to the basket during the 1987 finals against the Celtics. Johnson was the leader of the Lakers team.

15

A NEW ERA

After the Magic-Bird **era** of the 1980s, the Celtics and the Lakers didn't meet in the finals again until 2008. Fans could hardly wait! The Celtics lineup featured the "Big Three" of Kevin Garnett, Ray Allen, and Paul Pierce. The Lakers were led by possibly the best player in the world: Kobe Bryant.

The Boston **trio** proved to be too powerful to be stopped, and the Celtics won the title. In the sixth and final game, the Celtics crushed the Lakers by 39 points, 131–92. In that game, Allen tied an NBA finals record by hitting seven three-pointers.

Los Angeles would soon get another chance to beat their rivals when they met Boston in the 2010 finals. With the series tied at three games each, it all came down to one last game. At the end of the third quarter, Boston led, 57–53. Could the Lakers pull it out? Kobe Bryant scored 10 points in the fourth quarter, and the Lakers won! They beat the Celtics, 83–79, for the title.

Celtic Ray Allen drives the ball against Derek Fisher during the 2010 finals. The Lakers won their third championship against Boston that year.

EAST VS. WEST

Why is the rivalry between the Lakers and Celtics so much fun to watch? One reason is the incredible player matchups that have taken place over the years, such as Magic versus Bird.

The fact that the cities are so different is another reason why the rivalry is such a classic. Los Angeles is home to Hollywood and celebrities. Boston is an older, New England city on the opposite side of the country.

A ship sails into Boston Harbor. Boston is one of the nation's oldest cities. Los Angeles (right) is home to Hollywood and the movie industry.

The championship team wins a trophy like this. The Celtics and Lakers have won more trophies than any other NBA team.

Maybe the biggest reason that the Celtics and the Lakers make such great rivals is simply because they've been the two most **successful** teams in the NBA. From the NBA's beginning in 1946 until 2012, the Celtics and Lakers have combined to win as many championships as all the other teams put together. With that kind of history, you can expect this great rivalry to keep fans entertained for a long time to come.

CELTICS vs. LAKERS TIMELINE

1959
The Celtics and the Lakers meet in the finals for the first time. Led by players such as Bob Cousy, Boston wins the series, four games to zero. The Celtics are coached by the legendary Red Auerbach.

1968
The Lakers add Wilt Chamberlain to the team. Fans get to watch the exciting matchup between Chamberlain and Boston's Bill Russell.

1969
The Celtics finish the decade by beating the Lakers in the finals. The Celtics win the NBA championship every year in the 1960s except for 1967.

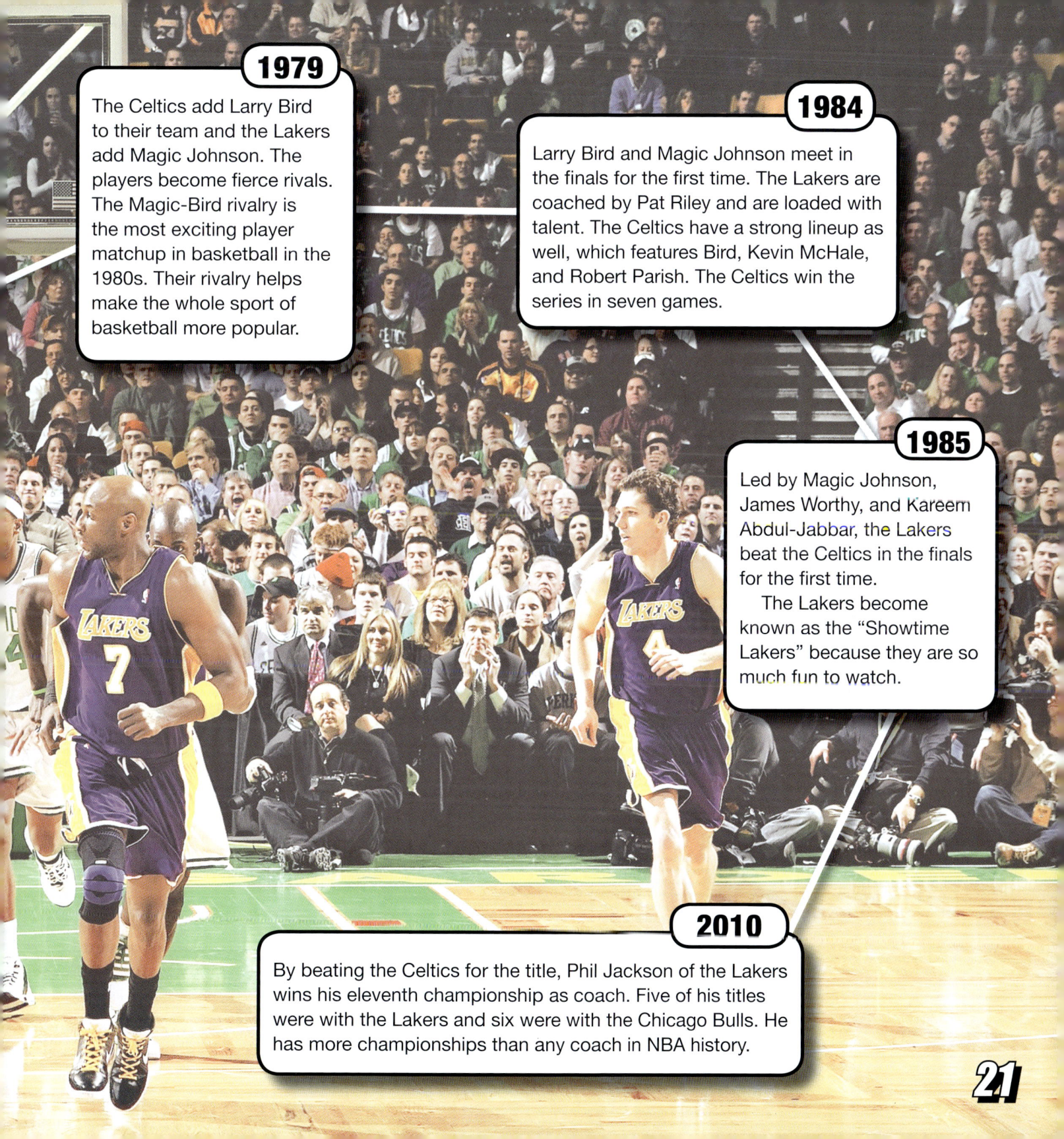

1979
The Celtics add Larry Bird to their team and the Lakers add Magic Johnson. The players become fierce rivals. The Magic-Bird rivalry is the most exciting player matchup in basketball in the 1980s. Their rivalry helps make the whole sport of basketball more popular.

1984
Larry Bird and Magic Johnson meet in the finals for the first time. The Lakers are coached by Pat Riley and are loaded with talent. The Celtics have a strong lineup as well, which features Bird, Kevin McHale, and Robert Parish. The Celtics win the series in seven games.

1985
Led by Magic Johnson, James Worthy, and Kareem Abdul-Jabbar, the Lakers beat the Celtics in the finals for the first time.

The Lakers become known as the "Showtime Lakers" because they are so much fun to watch.

2010
By beating the Celtics for the title, Phil Jackson of the Lakers wins his eleventh championship as coach. Five of his titles were with the Lakers and six were with the Chicago Bulls. He has more championships than any coach in NBA history.

CELTICS-LAKERS HEAD-TO-HEAD

	Celtics	**Lakers**
Team Location	Boston, Massachusetts	Los Angeles, California
Date Founded	1946	1947
Stadium Capacity	18,624	19,079
Number of Championships	17	16
Conference Titles	21	32
Primary Team Colors	Green and White	Purple and Gold
Most Valuable Players*	4	4
	Bob Cousy: 1957	Kareem Abdul-Jabbar: 1971, '72, '74, '76, '77, '80
	Bill Russell: 1958, '61, '62, '63, '65	Magic Johnson: 1987, '89, '90
	Dave Cowens: 1973	Shaquille O'Neal: 2000
	Larry Bird: 1984, '85, '86	Kobe Bryant: 2008

*The MVP award is given to one player in the league each year.

GLOSSARY

CENTURIES (SEN-Tshuh-reez) Periods of 100 years.

DECADE (DEH-kayd) A period of 10 years.

DESPERATELY (DES-puh-rit-lee) Wanting very much to do something.

DOMINANT (DAH-muh-nunt) Being the best at something, such as a game.

DYNASTY (DY-nus-tee) A period of time when a sports team wins a lot of championships.

ERA (EH-ruh) A specific period of time.

IMMIGRANTS (IH-muh-grunts) People from one country who come to live in another.

INTENSE (in-TENTS) Something done with lots of energy and feeling.

LOGO (LOH-goh) An official sign of an organization.

MYTHICAL (MITH-uh-kul) Something that is made-up and imaginary.

REVENGE (rih-VENJ) Getting even with someone.

RIVALRY (RY-vul-ree) Competition between teams that play each other a lot and feel strongly about winning.

SUCCESSFUL (SUK-SES-ful) Being good at something.

TRIO (TREE-oh) Three of something.

ULTIMATE (UL-tuh-mit) One of the best at something.

INDEX

A
Abdul-Jabbar, Kareem, 8, 13, 21
Allen, Ray, 16, 17

B
Baylor, Elgin, 10
Big Three, 16
Bird, Larry, 4, 6, 12, 14, 16, 18, 21
Boston, Massachusetts, 4, 6, 7, 10, 13, 14, 16, 18, 20
Bryant, Kobe, 8, 9, 16

C
competition, 4, 12

D
dynasty, 10

E
Eastern Conference, 8

F
finals, 4, 8, 10, 12, 13, 14, 16, 20, 21

G
Garnett, Kevin, 6, 16

J
Johnson, Magic, 4, 8, 12, 13, 14, 21

L
Los Angeles, California, 4, 8, 10, 14, 16, 18

O
O'Neal, Shaquille, 8, 9

P
Pierce, Paul, 16

Q
quarter, 16

R
Russell, Bill, 6, 11, 20

S
series, 12, 16

W
West, Jerry, 10
Western Conference, 8

WEBSITES

Due to the changing nature of Internet links, PowerKids Press has developed an online list of websites related to the subject of this book. This site is updated regularly. Please use this link to access the list:
www.powerkidslinks.com/sgr/lakcel/